LANDFORMS

GLACIERS

SANDY SEPEHRI

Rourke
Publishing LLC
Vero Beach, Florida 32964

www.rourkepublishing.com

Photo Credits
Pg. 4 © Svetlana Privezentseva; Pg. 5 © Xavier MARCHANT; Pg. 6a © Jeff Goldman; Pg. 6b © Jan Martin Will; Pg. 7 © Jan Martin Will; Pg. 8 © Jerome Scholler; Pg. 9a © SDC; Pg. 9b © Marc Pagani Photography; Pg. 10a- Lukás Hejtman; Pg. 10b © Vera Bogaerts; Pg. 11a © Maria Veras; Pg. 11b © Vassiliy Mikhailin; Pg. 12a © SDC; Pg. 12b © Andrew Lewis; Pg. 14 © Andrew Lewis; Pg. 15 © Basov Mikhail; Pg. 16 © Ulrike Hammerich; Pg. 17 © Galyna Andrushko; Pg. 18 © Matt Cooper; Pg. 19 © Scott Edlin; Pg. 20a © Ulrike Hammerich; Pg. 20b © Vera Bogaerts; Pg. 21a © USFS; Pg. 21b © USFS; Pg. 22a © Kenneth Spo; Pg. 22b © Vassiliy Mikhailin; Pg. 23a © Mark; Pg. 23b © Jozef Sedmak; Pg. 24a © Mike Norton; Pg. 24b © Tan, Kim Pin; Pg. 25a © Pedro Miguel Nunes; Pg. 25b © TAOLMOR; Pg. 25c © Don Wilkie; Pg. 26a © Josef F. Stuefer; Pg. 26b © Ulrike Hammerich; Pg. 27a © Keith Levit; Pg. 27b © Gail Johnson; Pg. 28a © Ferenc Cegledi; Pg. 28b © Jason Smith; Pg. 28c © Peter Kunasz; Pg. 28d © Keith Levit; Pg. 29a © Eric Gevaert; Pg. 29b © EGD

Pg. 30 Illustration by Erik Courtney

Design and Production - Blue Door Publishing; bdpublishing.com

Library of Congress Cataloging-in-Publication Data

Sepehri, Sandy.
  Glaciers / Sandy Sepehri.
    p. cm. -- (Landforms)
  ISBN 978-1-60044-544-6 (hard cover)
  ISBN 978-1-60044-705-1 (soft cover)
  1. Glaciers--Juvenile literature. I. Title.
  GB2403.8.S47 2008
  551.31'2--dc22

                                    2007012143

Printed in the USA

IG/IG

Table of Contents

What Is a Glacier?

A glacier is a huge piece of ice on land, made from snow that has accumulated for hundreds, or thousands of years. A small glacier can be the size of two football fields and a large glacier can cover an area of more than 30,000 square miles (48,280 km). The largest glacier in the world, the Antarctic ice sheet, covers about 98 percent of Antarctica— the fifth largest continent on Earth.

When glaciers melt they form lakes.

ANTARCTICA

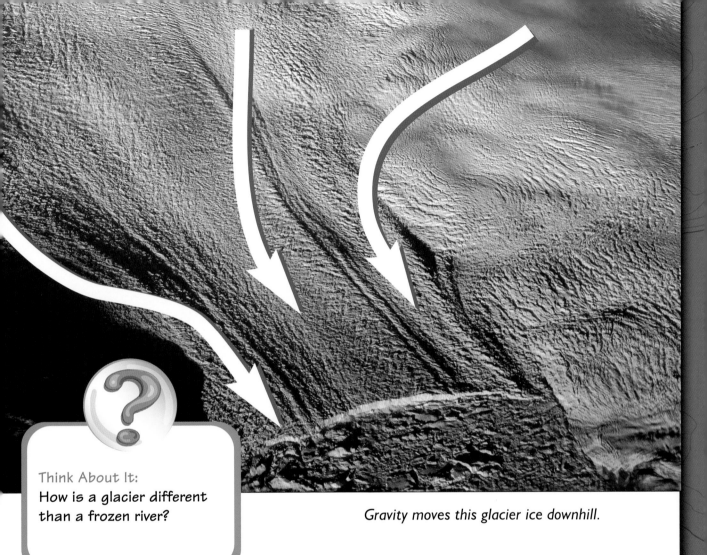

Think About It:
How is a glacier different than a frozen river?

Gravity moves this glacier ice downhill.

A glacier is not simply a body of water that has frozen. Glaciers are made after many years of snow have been pressed into ice. Another difference glaciers have from other bodies of frozen water is that they move. What makes them move is their massive size and weight, combined with the force of gravity. Glaciers flow slowly down mountains, across plains, and out to sea, where they break off into icebergs.

Where to Find Glaciers

Glaciers can only form where the winters have snow and the summers are cold enough to preserve it. Since temperatures get colder at higher **altitudes** on Earth, most glaciers form on high mountaintops and in the Polar Regions. There are glaciers on every continent, except Australia. What varies, from continent to continent is the altitude at which glaciers are found.

The top of this mountain is 13,500 feet (4,115 m).

This glacier in Antarctica formed at sea level.

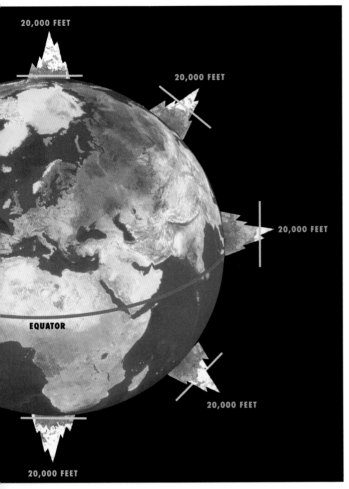

20,000 FEET

20,000 FEET

20,000 FEET

EQUATOR

20,000 FEET

20,000 FEET

At the top and bottom of the Earth, glaciers form at lower altitudes.

Generally, glaciers occur above the snow line and where summers are cold enough to preserve winter snow. Not all snow lines occur at the same altitude. Near the equator, which is warm because it is in the path of the sun's rays, the snow line doesn't occur until an altitude of about 16,000 feet (5,100 m), more than three miles (4.8 km) above sea level. At the South Pole, however, which is cold because it is tilted away from the sun's rays, the snow line occurs at sea level.

Did You Know?
Glaciers cover 10 percent of the Earth. If they were all put together, they'd cover South America.

A Closer Look

They may become giants, but all glaciers begin from tiny snowflakes. In cold areas, years of snowflakes become buried and compressed under new piles of snowfall. Under the weight of the added snow, delicate snowflakes break apart and are reshaped into rounded grains resembling sugar. As the compression continues, the grains enter a stage between snow and ice, called firn, which, after a few years, turns into glacial ice.

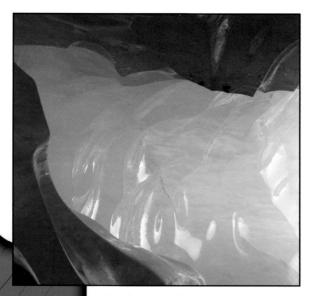

Sunlight makes its way deep within a glacier ice cave.

Layers of a Glacier

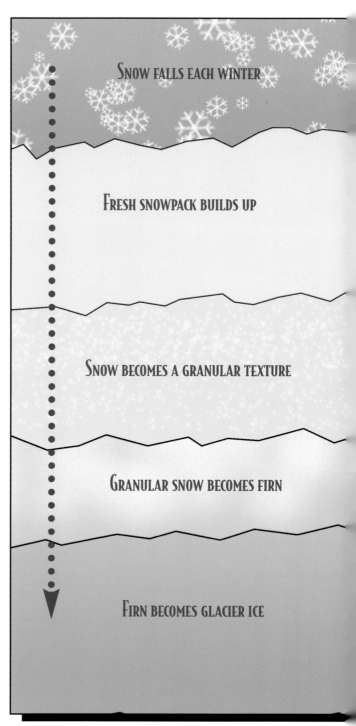

SNOW FALLS EACH WINTER

FRESH SNOWPACK BUILDS UP

SNOW BECOMES A GRANULAR TEXTURE

GRANULAR SNOW BECOMES FIRN

FIRN BECOMES GLACIER ICE

Accumulation Zone

The upper part of a glacier, where most of the snowfall collects, is called the **accumulation zone**, representing 60-70 percent of its surface. This zone includes an area of permanent snow cover, called a snowfield. Deep cracks occur in the snowfield, resulting from a glacier's change in speed. These cracks are called **crevasses.** Looking into a crevasse, a **glaciologist** can see the different layers of ice formed from snowfall each year.

Crevasse

This crevasse is deep and dangerous. Every year there are reports of climbers falling into these cracks. Climbers can be injured or killed.

Glacier Terminus

Sitting on top of the earth's bedrock is the bottom section of a glacier, called the ablation zone. The base of the **ablation zone** has several names, including face, snout, foot, toe, and terminus. Like a bulldozer's blade, the terminus pushes along everything in the glacier's path, and moves objects, such as large boulders, far from their original locations. These transported boulders are called erratic boulders because they look out of place with their new environment.

What is the only continent that has no glaciers? Australia.

Glacier Terminus

The **terminus** is the part of a glacier that shows how quickly it's moving. As the terminus pushes along everything in the glacier's path, soil and small rocks are scraped into piles called **moraines** which collect along the bottom and sides of the glacier. The terminus can also move over the edge of land and hang over water, where large pieces break off, or calve, into icebergs.

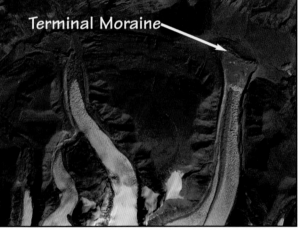

Terminal Moraine

This satellite photograph shows a moraine that was created by a glacier.

Icebergs break away from a glacier's terminus and float until they melt.

Types of Glaciers

There are many types of glaciers, each named for their shape or location. The two main categories are **continental glaciers** (also called ice sheets) and mountain glaciers (also called **alpine** glaciers). Continental glaciers are gigantic slabs of ice spread over a continent, found only at the South and North Poles. The part that reaches over the edge of land and floats on top of the ocean is called an ice shelf.

Continental glacier.

Mountain glacier.

Q: What is the difference between a glacier and an iceberg?
A: A glacier is on land and an iceberg is in water. Icebergs break off from glaciers that flow over the water's edge.

Parts of this glacier are falling off into the water, creating icebergs.

The Greenland ice sheet.

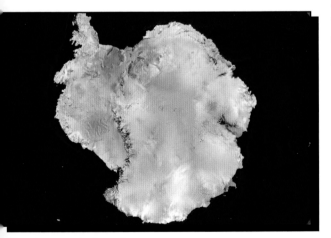

The Antarctic ice sheet.

Ice Sheets

Ice sheets contain about 90 percent of the world's ice and about 75 percent of the world's fresh water. The Greenland ice sheet is so large, if it were to melt, it would make ocean levels all over the world rise up almost 20 feet (6 m), about the size of a two-story house. If the much larger Antarctic ice sheet were to melt, world ocean levels would rise about 220 feet (67 m)—the height of a city skyscraper!

GLACIER TRIVIA

Did you know the Antarctic ice sheet has been on Earth for 40 million years? It is so heavy it pushes down parts of Antarctica more than one mile (1.6 km) below sea level!

Ice Caps

A much smaller version of an ice sheet is an **ice cap**, positioned on top of a mountain, like a hat. When ice caps and ice sheets flow into the sea, they create ice streams—areas of faster flowing ice.

Smaller than ice caps are ice fields. Unlike other glaciers, an ice field's rate of ice flow is determined by the conditions of the ground beneath it, such as its shape and temperature.

A large ice field runs several hundred miles

Mountain Glaciers

Mountain glaciers occur all over the world. The most common is the **cirque glacier**, a semicircular slab of ice, located high on the side of a mountain. A cirque glacier is formed in a bowl-shaped mountain groove, also called a cirque. Occasionally several cirques will form around the same mountain. When three or more cirques encircle a mountain, they form a sharp peak called a horn.

The red line in this photo shows a cirque glacier.

Cirque Glacier

This satellite photo shows what remains of a cirque glacier thousands of years old.

Can you say cirque? (SIRK)
A mountainside with a semicircular hollow and steep walls formed by glacial erosion.

Valley Glaciers

A **valley glacier** is also named for its location. It creeps slowly down a mountain, towards a mountain valley—the lowland between mountains. The Rocky Mountains, in the Western United States, have about 50 valley glaciers. As valley glaciers slide down, they drag along sharp rocks and ice, cutting the valley sides and floor into a U-shape. The Yosemite Valley in California is an example of a U-shaped valley.

Glaciers carve out large sections of rock as they move forward creating a U-shaped valley.

Valley Glaciers

Several valley glaciers are clearly shown in this satellite photo taken over Alaska.

A climber makes his way across a Piedmont Glacier.

Piedmont Glaciers

When valley glaciers flow to the base of mountains, they can combine together on land and form a thick, circular sheet of ice, called a **piedmont glacier**. The largest glacier in Alaska, the Malaspina Glacier, is also the world's largest piedmont glacier. It spreads across a coastal plain, covering 1,500 square miles (2,414 km), and is more than a mile thick.

Piedmont Glacier

Valley Glacier

Seen from above, a piedmont glacier resembles a frying pan. The 'handle' is the column of ice connecting the piedmont glacier to the valley glacier that flows down the mountain.

How Glaciers Move

Even when part of a huge glacier, ice and snow are easily deformed by the stress of weight and pressure. Once glacial ice becomes 60 feet (18 m) thick, it is heavy enough to move. Glaciers can move from a few inches a day to more than a hundred feet a day. The underside of a glacier moves more slowly than its top portion, because of the friction it makes as its rubs across the surface of the ground.

This glacier moves slow enough that people can walk in front of it without being hurt by its movement.

A slow moving glacier.

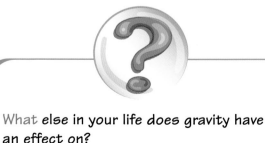

What else in your life does gravity have an effect on?

A fast moving glacier.

This glacier is on a steep hillside and its movement can easily hurt or kill you.

The pressure that makes a glacier move comes from the force of gravity upon its mass. Glaciers show two kinds of motion. The more dramatic of the two is the ice avalanche, which occurs when a hanging glacier drops from a steep mountainside. Usually, glaciers surge slowly along the ground. The movement of a valley glacier, for example, ranges from less than an inch to a few feet a day.

Besides their mass and gravity, glacier movement is affected by climate. Being made of ice, parts of glaciers will melt in warm climates. Melted glacial water is called meltwater.

Meltwater flows toward the base of a glacier. It travels in tunnels inside a glacier, and sometimes in channels on the surface. Meltwater streams along on the ground, next to a glacier, and can flow out to sea or form lakes.

Glacier lakes form from glacier meltwater.

When a glacier collects more snow and ice than it loses to melting, it advances, or pushes downhill. In a warmer climate, when it loses snow and ice to melting, it appears to move backward, or retreat.

When the amount of its new snow is balanced with what melts, a glacier becomes stationary.

The Grinnell Glacier in Montana has been retreating for several years.

The Grinnell Glacier in 1981.

The Grinnell Glacier in 2006.

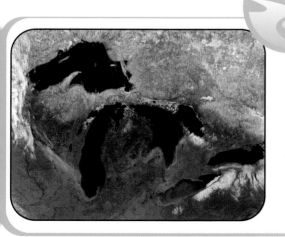

The Great Lakes (*Superior, Michigan, Huron, Ontario, and Erie*), are between the United States and Canada. They were formed 10,000 years ago by meltwater from a retreating ice sheet.

Many geologic features are created by glaciers. They are identified in three groups: erosional landforms, depositional landforms, and ice features. Erosional landforms are created as glaciers **erode**, or wear away, parts of mountains as they slide down and drag along rocks. These include grooves, hanging valleys, and tarns—lakes made by glaciers. Depositional landforms are made from glacial deposits, meaning the layers of rocks, gravel, and sand they leave behind as they pass.

Think About It:
As the Earth warms and glaciers retreat, how will this affect the people and animals who rely on them?

Erosional Landforms

Yosemite Valley is a well known area that has been carved out by glaciers.

Depositional Landforms

A retreating glacier left these huge terminus mounds behind the Teton Mountains in Wyoming.

Ice Features

Glaciers break into pieces as they move forward, creating large, falling chunks of ice.

Ice features are structures made from ice, including cirque glaciers, valley glaciers, crevasses, and icefalls (rapidly flowing portions of some glaciers). An icefall is a downhill flow from a steep slope. The flow of an icefall is many times faster than average glacial flow. This rapid flow fractures the ice, forming crevasses.

Fresh water flows from a melting glacier.

How Glaciers Benefit People

Glaciers are a natural resource. Unlike ocean water, glacial meltwater is not salty and can be used for drinking and watering crops. Meltwater irrigates crops and is used for drinking water in India, Afghanistan, Pakistan, Nepal, South America, and China during their dry seasons. The peak period for collecting glacial meltwater is in early summer. The surge of melting can make streams of water erupt from the base of a glacier, often flooding the valley below.

This train runs on electricity. You can see the cable above the engine.

For hundreds of years, Swiss farmers have benefited from glaciers by channeling meltwater to their crops. Another benefit from glaciers is electricity. The power released by the surge of glacial melting is harnessed for generating **hydroelectricity**. In Canada, Europe, and New Zealand scientists and engineers use meltwater to generate hydroelectricity. In Switzerland, the railway system is powered by hydroelectricity.

Each year in the United States, millions of tourists visit Glacier National Park, a 16,000 square mile (25,000 km) setting, located in the state of Montana.

In Europe, the Aletsch Glacier is a major tourist site. It's known for the dark stripes running down its entire length, called a **medial moraine**, resulting from soil and sediment pushed together by converging ice fields.

Sediment flows along with the glacier ice at a very slow pace.

Sediment

Looking down on a glacier from a satellite we are able to see how the sediment creates a medial moraine.

Sediment

Life Among Glaciers

A variety of animal life has adapted to living among glaciers. Antarctic penguins protect themselves with their tight plumage (feathers). The Arctic fox and Arctic hare camouflage themselves by turning their coats from brown to white to match the snow—so they won't be easily seen by predators. Small rodents adapt by increasing their metabolic rate and body heat and taking shelter under the snow cover.

Arctic fox in winter.

The Arctic hare blends in with the snow.

Arctic fox in summer.

Other Arctic animals include the grey wolf, the muskox, and the caribou. In the Alpine regions, the stone ibex and chamois are adapted for climbing the steep, rocky hillsides.

Muskox

Caribou

Mountain Goat

In North American mountains are dahl sheep and mountain goats, and in the flatter areas are moose, elk, and bears. Looking down from the sky are many kinds of birds, including the eagle.

The largest carnivore on land is the polar bear, which lives in the Arctic. Its white fur provides camouflage and its thick layer of blubber provides insulation.

Glaciers and Global Warming

Glacial melting is an important indicator of global warming. Global warming refers to the rising temperature of the Earth, partly caused by pollution that comes from power plants and automobiles, called greenhouse gases. Scientists warn that, unless this warming trend is reversed, global disasters will follow, including melting glaciers, rising sea levels, flooding coasts, droughts, wildfires, disruption of ecosystems, and the extinction of animal species.

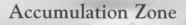

Accumulation Zone

Valley
Glacier

Glacier

Medial
Moraine

Cirque
Glacier

Piedmont Glacier

Crevasses

Glacier Terminus

Glacier
Lake

Terminal Moraine

Glossary

ablation zone (AB uh la shun ZOHN) — the area of a glacier below the snowline that receeds faster than it grows

accumulation zone (uh KYOO myuh shun ZOHN) — an area on a mountain where snow piles up in large quantities

alpine (AL pin) — the high area of a mountain or mountain range that is above the treeline

altitude (AL ti tood) — the height of something usually measured above sea level

cirque glacier (SIRK GLAY shur) — a bowl shaped area on the side of a mountain that holds snow year round

continental glacier (KON tuh nuhnt el GLAY shur) — glaciers that form over entire continents like Antarctica

crevasse (krev VAS) — a deep crack in glacier ice or snow

erode (i RODE) — to wear or wash away

glacier lake (GLAY shur LAKE) — a lake formed by a melting glacier

glaciologist (glay SHOL ah jist) — a person who studies the formation and movement of ice and glaciers

hydroelectricity (hye droh i lek TRISS uh tee) — electricity created by the use of water power

ice cap (EYESS kap) — the top of a mountain that is covered by ice

medial moraine (MEE dee uahl muh RAN) — an area of dirt and rock that forms when two glaciers come together

piedmont glacier (PED mont GLAY shur) — a valley glacier that has run onto flat ground and spread out

terminus (TUR muh nus) — the end of a glacier

valley glacier (VAL ee GLAY shur) — a glacier that occupies the valley between mountains

Index

Further Reading

Bodden, Valerie. *Glaciers, Our World.* Creative Education, 2006.
Carruthers, Margaret. *Glaciers.* Watts Library, 2005.
Higgins, Nadia. *Welcome to Glacier National Park.* Child's World, 2006.

Websites To Visit

www.nsidc.org/glaciers/
www.42explore.com/glaciers.htm
www.sciencenewsforkids.org/articles/20050914/refs.asp

About The Author

Sandy Sepehri lives with her husband, Shahram, and their three children in Florida. She has a bachelor's degree and writes freelance articles and children's stories. She has also written a number of fiction and nonfiction books.